From Glory to Glory

MIRIAM CAULEY-CRISP

From Glory to Glory

Scripture

2 Corinthians 3:18

And we all, who with unveiled faces contemplate the LORD's glory, are being transformed into his image with ever-increasing glory, which comes from the LORD, who is the Spirit.

Dedication

This book is dedicated to the Father, Son and Holy Spirit.

This book was also written in honor of my mother Lucille Toney

Copyrighted Material

No part of this book shall be reproduced or transmitted in any form by any means, electronic, mechanical, magnetic and photographic including photocopying, recording or by any information storage and retrieval system, without the permission prior written permission of the author or publisher. No patent liability is assumed with respect to the use of the information contained herein. Although every precaution has been taken in the preparation of this book, the publisher and author assume no responsibility for errors or omissions. Neither is any liability assumed for damages resulting from the use of the information contained herein.

All Rights Reserved
Copyright © 2018 by Miriam Cauley-Crisp
ISBN-13: 978-1724365477
ISBN-10: 1724365479

Table of Contents

Scripture

Dedication

Preface

Prayer has been the foundation

Introduction

Chapter 1

Loyalty of a Virtuous Leader................................16

Chapter 2

The Beginning Moments....................................20

Chapter 3

The Sharing Group...22

Chapter 4

Elevation..26

Chapter 5

Higher Calling..29

Chapter 6

Troubles Don't Last Always................................31

Chapter 7

Stepping into Another Real..................................35

Chapter 8

Annual Conference…………………………………….39

Chapter 9

Well Done My Servant……………………….............42

A Word To Stand On (Excerpts)

Morning Glory

Acknowledgements

About The Author

Preface

For as long as I can remember; prayer has always been the rooted standing ground of my foundation along with the principles of righteousness. As a child; I remember hearing sounds of continuous spiritual warfare, travailing, praise and worship, intercession and spiritual tongues going forth, whatever manner it took in making our supplication known unto God. Often, I may not have understood what was being stirred then; because I was looking at things one-dimensional from a natural standpoint, but there was an unquestionable stirring in the spiritual realm. I knew just to being in the midst of the prayers gave my natural being intellect while it awakened me spiritually. Regardless of what religion one may be, prayer is universal. It's a good thing and necessary for everyone in everyday life. The bible mandates *1 Thessalonians 5:17* Pray without ceasing. Prayer is vital and apart of building a solid relationship and staying connected to God.

I was brought up in a Christian Holy Ghost filled church where invocation of prayer was a common and remained in the forefront, it was also consistently carried out within the walls of my home. It was an ever-present position.

Regardless of where prayer took place, evidence had proven to me that God meets us and answer prayers no matter where we are.

Nevertheless, I do know the prayer life I observed in the privacy of my home stated a personal involvement, a more intimate encounter, it was training ground; to spiritually prepare and equip me to come into the knowledge of who God is for myself. Having been surrounded by an overflow of endless prayers, one thing I do know is I had a true prayer warrior on the battlefield interceding on my behalf day in and day out covering and undergirding the souls of God's people for many years, who walked in holy boldness under the authority of the Holy Ghost.

One who intervened, labored and travailed, who understood and truly knew how to warfare in the spirit. One who instilled in me that once a supplication was made known unto God – begin to walk in Expectancy! One who imparted in me the results and importance of fasting, praying remaining steadfast and how to lean not unto my own understanding but how to really trust in God by way of demonstration.

A mantle has been passed, as the carrier and fruit of that tree, I am held accountable to share the story of a woman's walk in the ministry and to ensure that the Glory of the Lord be magnified through her story. I am blessed to have been able to bear witness to the manifestation of all that was labored for in the spiritual realm, and attest to countless signs, miracles and wonders of God's promises.

Prayer has been the Foundation

Prayer, a solemn request for help or expression of thanks; it's our way to communicate to God. Do you have a solid prayer life? Do you believe in the power of prayer? How does one pray effectively and get results? Prayer is spiritual and takes place in the spirit realm. There are various traditional types, acts and styles of praying according to what ones' religious beliefs. Praying is deemed to offer hope and strength while waiting. Prayer is diverse and universal.

However, as Christians, we pray to God who is our Heavenly Father. We go before Him in prayer with an act of Adoration, Contrition, Intercession, Petition, or Thanksgiving. These acts of prayer must come from a sincere heart and should be carried out with a spirit of humility as it is meant to be a two-way dialogue with God.

While in God's presence, it is very important that we listen for His voice. Having faith and believing is our response to God while waiting on the petition of our prayers to manifest as well as assuring it aligns with God's will for our lives. We must also learn to remove self out of the way and allow Him to complete the work. No battle is ever our own, it belongs to the Lord to fight. Once we pray about a thing, we should leave all cares at the altar. There is a saying; "if we pray why worry, if we worry why pray", there is no need to confuse or waver in our faith especially after we have petitioned our requests. God promises in His word, ***James 1:6*** *But let him ask in faith, nothing wavering. For he that wavereth is like a wave of the sea driven with the wind and tossed.*

As Christian believers of God's word, we must begin to let go and let God. Whatever we ask in prayer begin to expect. What God promises in His word settles any debate any day. The bible declares, ***Matthew 21:22*** *And all things, whatsoever ye shall ask in prayer, believing, ye shall receive.*

God's love cascades all around us that He is mindful of our needs before we even recognize there was ever a lack. He blesses us even without us sending up a specific request or any formal act of prayer. He knows all and sees all. He is Sovereign, and He is in the blessing business. Even when we are sinning He yet still blesses us. His grace and mercy surround our borders without our knowing.

Think about it! Perhaps your day to day does not encompass having some form of prayer life yet you're reaping the benefits of someone else's prayers; then there must be a prayer warrior behind the veil covering and interceding on your behalf.

If you do not already have a prayer life, I encourage you to develop a consistent one. It is essential when you're expecting to prosper and see the move of God. Igniting your prayer life will surely transform your spiritual perspective for it is foundational.

Introduction

You see, I had a praying Mother!!! This book **From Glory to Glory** is a factual testimonial account that expounds on the life and legacy of my mom Pastor Lucille Toney, her spiritual walk with God and the multi-faceted mantle she left.

This spiritual inspirational read will detail her fruitful work of labor, her dedication, obedience, faithfulness, wisdom, and her admired strength as a woman in the ministry. It will also highlight her service as a philanthropist and spiritual relationships to the countless lives she touched until God called her home to rest in Glory.

As a witness to her many assignments, this is my personal descriptive account of my mother's spiritual legacy. Kinship to this mighty Woman of God is a privilege and a blessing to have had such an anointed influential model who secured a relationship with God in every area of her life.

My desire is that the reader connects in such a way that the anointing flows and a spiritual impartation begins to take place. The reader will gain spiritual insight, encouragement and encounter such an overall Godly life-changing experience. One will also witness the unfailing love for God from a servant whose life reflected His living word.

Chapter 1

Loyalty of a Virtuous Leader
The Gifts

Pastor Lucille Toney was an empowering kingdom builder with over 35 years in ministry who operated under the fivefold ministry (Apostle, Prophet, Evangelist, Pastor and Teacher) and remained faithful to her God-given office titles, as a Teacher, Evangelist, Prophetess and an ordained Pastor. She flowed under a heavy prophetic deliverance mantle. As a visionary leader, she had such a strong sense of spiritual discernment. Her powerful anointing from God exposed the enemy's tactics and brought deliverance to those who were bound. Her Christian ministerial path reflected a walk of transparency, she was radical for Christ and often shared the goodness of the Lord everywhere she'd go. Pastor Lucille Toney was known as being an anointed intercessor, powerful prayer warrior and spiritual confidant. For many years she encouraged individuals to not remain at the same level but to embrace spiritual elevation. As a humble leader, her assertiveness and holy boldness helped educate, equip and empower hundreds of people from all walks of life. She believed in Holiness and living a life that was pleasing before God.

My mother was a true virtuous Woman of God, she was always steadfast, orderly and obedient under the authority of the Holy Ghost. I witnessed my mother laboring many days fasting, praying and tarrying before God. She stayed on the wall until her prayers manifested. She endured patience as she did not mind waiting, because she knew in the end it shall speak.

Habakkuk 2:3 *And the LORD answered me, and said, Write the vision, and make it plain upon tables, that he may run that readeth it.* For the vision *is* yet for an appointed time, but at the end it shall speak, and not lie: though it tarry, wait for it; because it will surely come, it will not tarry.

    She was a woman who had a mind to serve and live righteous for Christ, an ear to listen and harkened diligently to His voice as she only moved by the instructions of His spirit. She was a woman who had solid unwavering water walking faith and she was sensitive by way of God's direction. By example, she demonstrated the epitome of a servant sharing a wealth of wisdom and guidance. She was indeed a woman who was after God's own heart.

A woman who wore many hats both natural and spiritual and carried out meaningful relationships to a multitude of individuals. However, those relationships were incomparable to the personal relationship she had with the Lord. She was very passionate about her bond with Christ. I'm talking about a woman who had a made-up mind that once she committed her life to serve God, there was no turning back. It took some shaking, shaping and molding.

I am sure there were several instances where she was tested by circumstances that could have caused her to backslide, but she was committed.

It is challenging at times walking a straight and narrow, but she was not moved by temporary circumstances when she had acquired such a permanent faith in God that moved mountains.

Her loyalty to God was unquestionable she trusted Him wholeheartedly with her life. Whatever she endured she trusted God for her Victory. She stood on His word daily until each scripture came into fruition. That's the type of faith she had with the Lord.

Regardless of what, she believed His Word! The Lord had proven to my mom time and time again, His word was His promise and because of her obedience for being a frontline willing vessel to do His will; she received an overflow portion of His blessings, I'm talking about **Deuteronomy 28** blessed. She was persistent in honoring His commands and was blessed for her obedience.

Chapter 2

*The Beginning Moments
Coming into the knowledge*

Pastor Lucille Toney always acquired a desire and love for God. Her desire to know God for herself was embedded early on in life. As a child, she attended Simuel Baptist Church faithfully with family. Beyond this; her eagerness for God continued.

June 15, 1967, she married my father Ben Cauley Jr., to this union four daughters were born Chekita, Shuronda, Monica and Miriam. She united with her husband and joined his home church at New Friendship Missionary Baptist Church under the leadership of Rev. W.M. Brown, where she was a faithful member for many years. It is noted that this was the beginning moments and the making of her dedication that established her coming into the knowledge of Christ. As a young woman, she must have been strong-willed with a mindset to want to serve and be in the midst of God's presence at such a youthful age.

By the early 1980's she and my father divorced. The result of this shift required her to make some uncompromising decisions. Having four daughters to support and additional needs to meet; she remained prayerful and persevered to regain constant strength to endure the many hurdles she encountered thereafter. This is said to have been the beginning moments of several adversities she faced. Despite obstacles her faith remained strong. Her resilience to bounce back was undeniably a reflection of her dignity. My mom was such a woman of elegance, with a smile on her face, she kept her composure during difficulties, her reaction to every action resulted in prayer.

Even after the divorce, she remained faithful to God while planting and growing her seed of faith. During this hurdle, it taught her tenacity and how to keep moving forward against all odds. She became an unstoppable force and blazed the trail full speed ahead trusting God in all things. Her solid foundation was built many years before her ministry walk ever began.

Chapter 3

The Sharing Group
Building Spiritual Connections

Pastor Lucille Toney withdrew her membership at New Friendship MBC and joined Monumental Baptist Church under the leadership of Rev. Samuel Kyles. During this time, I was of age to recall a lot of what took place. During her tenure at Monumental, she continued to build her faith and relationship with God. Wherever God led her to fellowship, she remained faithful until she completed her assignment.

Attending church was routine for my mother. It became a part of her and was her place of refuge. Being in the house of the Lord was a covering for her, it was as common to her as going to work daily. She had to be in the house of the Lord, and there I was; along with my sisters in church as well. Faithfully! But simply going to church wasn't enough, she felt there was more to do within the church.

As I reflect; I recall her being very active at Monumental, she carried out many roles, from choir member, consistently attending mid-week service orchestrating events, to becoming a committee member of the birthday club and other church office committees. Even as a small child, I saw how spiritually dedicated she was and her eagerness when it came to the things of God.

She was always about God's business. Whenever she saw work that needed to be done, without procrastination there she was laboring doing the work of the Lord.

Luke 10:2 *The harvest is plenty, but the laborers are few.*

While at Monumental Baptist Church, several relationships were built, and many spiritual connections had been birthed. Through building meaningful relationships and continuing her walk with the Lord, He began to lead her into a ministerial path. She started her work in an outreach ministry called The Sharing Group under the leadership of Rev. C. Thomas. This was a small faith-based ministry where Christian believers would gather often over each other's house to fellowship, intercede, plan family events, outreach functions, have bible study, discuss personal calling and ministry work and simply share the goodness of the Lord. The sharing group was a gateway for her to awaken and recognize that there was a greater assignment in her.

The word declares, ***Acts 2:44-47** All the believers were together and had everything in common. They sold property and possessions to give to anyone who had need. ⁴⁶Every day they continued to meet together in the temple courts. They broke bread in their homes and ate together with glad and sincere hearts, praising God and enjoying the favor of all the people. And the Lord added to their number daily those who were being saved.*

As her ministry walk began to enlarge; so, did the perspective of her religious belief, therefore she shifted from Baptist to Non-denominational faith-based church; which resulted in her membership to All Believer's Christian Center under the leadership of Pastor Joyce Ray.

Spiritual growth began to accompany my mom in such a way that she was on fire for the Lord. I observed a different kind of kingdom work that was assigned to her hands. She learned how to be free in the Holy Spirit and experienced so many other spiritual planes in ministry and entered into heavenly realms of God. During her walk, her divine experience was to go higher in the Lord. She understood with each level came new levels of ministry.

Even after all that was witnessed spiritually, all the praying, fasting, laboring attesting to miracles performed at All Believers Christian Center, she kept saying, "There's more." My mom experienced a journey of being taken from Glory to Glory.

Chapter 4

Elevation
Entering A New Level

In the early 1990's, God began expanding her walk yet again, she began walking and operating in one of her many gifts and became head intercessor, armorbearer and operated in the prophetic, while under the leadership of Apostle Eunice Holman of Glory Ministries. My mom and Apostle Holman's friendship was birthed through the connection of the Sharing Group. They not only became really good friends outside of ministry; but they also operated, as a tag team in deliverance ministry, preaching the kingdom of God and casting out unclean spirits. She was one of the most dedicated faithful members while serving in this ministry. She was present and worked diligently every time the church doors were open. As a teenager, I recall her getting up early on Saturday mornings cleaning the church and preparing God's house for services on Sundays she made sure His house was constantly in order.

Often times, she would pray and just sit in His presence for several hours. After being gone awhile, I would sometimes call to ask where she was, she would say, "I'm still at the church baby". She was a generous giver with her time and had such an endowing love for God. Her loyalty to Him was selfless. She would always say, "what we do for Christ will last". The goal for her work of labor was to ultimately please Him.

Her evangelistic walk was not only carried out within the church but outside of the church walls. She served within the community by cultivating and edifying lives in outreach. I remember the times; my mom would go into the hospitals and nursing homes and visit the sick and sit with shut in and pray for the patients and their families. If anyone need a prayer to reach heaven, my mom was the one everyone called on. Her prayer life and relationship with God was so keen, it's like she had direct connection to Him. Whenever someone was ill and needed prayer for healing, she would always be depended upon to intercede on their behalf and speak healing. She was all about living out God's word. She won the trust of so many people.

There were many times she'd visit the inmates in jail pray with them and read scriptures, sharing the goodness of the Lord. She was zealous serving the people of God. She desired to see everyone win. During her ministry walk hundreds of souls were healed, saved, delivered and set free. She stayed on the wall for not only those she knew, but for total strangers as well. My mom was definitely an intercessor and a true dedicated soul winner.

The bible declares, ***James 5:14-15,*** *Is anyone among you sick? Let him call for the elders of the church, and let them pray over him, anointing him with oil in the name of the Lord. And the prayer of faith will save the one who is sick, and the Lord will raise him up. And if he has committed sins, he will be forgiven.*

Chapter 5

A Higher Calling
Ordination

After a long journey and commitment to her assignment, Pastor Lucille Toney became a phenomenal student while sitting diligently under the teaching of Apostle Eunice Holman at Glory Ministries. Her trustworthiness, her obedience to protocol and her dedication to her calling as an intercessor were great attributes for kingdom building, but God's will was to elevate her to an even higher calling. The fruits of her labor were rewarded.

Matthew 25:23 *Thou hast been faithful over a few things; I will make thee ruler over many things.*

In 1996, the spirit of the Lord led Apostle Holman to ordain her as elder and evangelist, although she had already carried the evangelistic anointing; she had become licensed to go out to speak and minister to the masses without any restrictions. She was fully equipped for the assignment. God continued to elevate her and use her mightily in every capacity during her ministerial path.

I remember as she began to go forth to minister at serval different engagements; I could sense the anointing and power of God all around her as she ministered under the authority of the Holy Ghost. Her flesh would decrease as the spirit of the Lord increased. I no longer saw her as my mother; but she had become my spiritual model.

Chapter 6

Troubles Don't Last Always
The Endurance

Pastor Lucille Toney had always been transparent about kingdom work and her relationship with the Lord. She stayed true to who she was in Him. However, her personal life and circumstances at home remained private. My mom was truly a long sufferer, she didn't mind waiting. She not only waited on God, but she waited in God. One of her favorite scriptures she stood on was **Psalm 46:10** *Be Still and know that I am God.*

In the midst of all the highlights of her operating in her calling in ministry, as a teenager, I remember my mom endured some difficult times behind closed doors. I didn't fully understand the depths of the obstacles or the challenging decisions she had to face, but because I was connected to her, I would always sense when there was a rise in pressure.

Being a single woman and mother, she never wanted her daughters to feel the wrath of her hardship. She never once wavered during the rage of the storm. She was grounded enough to bear the weight of her own cross. Her reaction to every action was to pray. That alone, had given her the strength required to hold on further. I remember she would go into her secret place which was her prayer closet and lay before God and didn't come out until she heard Him speak. Nevertheless, she believed and trusted God for everything that concerned her.

Psalms 91 *says, "He that dwelleth in the secret place of the most High, shall abide under the shadow of the Almighty.*

As a child I often recollect, walking through the house calling for my mom, looking in every room for her, whenever she didn't answer; I knew she would be in her secret place just sitting quietly before the Lord, behind the veil. My sister and I would sit quietly in her room and just listen to her pray until she would come out.

The beauty of it for me was, when the closet door opened, I knew she had been behind the veil in the presence of the Lord as there would be such a glow that surrounded her countenance; that's how I knew the spirit of the Lord met her there in her secret place. I would hear her not only petition a prayer to manifest for herself, but she interceded on behalf of others as well, bridging the gaps calling out their names, praying that God perform miracles in the lives. She was a covering for those who were connected to her. Her prayers were selfless, it was never about her, but about souls. She represented the epitome of a true Christian Woman of God.

In addition to fasting and praying, I observed my mom consistently apply acts of holiness such as being a consistent tither, anointing with oil and studying the word of God to maintain a solid relationship with the Lord. This account was observed years before she even accepted her calling in the ministry.

All in all, during her obstacles, she never gave up gave in nor threw in the towel. God has always been her sole provider. Every attack was fought by waiting patiently on God and standing on the promises of His word. One would had never known all that she had endured. Beyond her contagious smile was years of disappointment but she yet remained faithful doing the Lord's will amid her adversities. Whatever fiery dart the enemy tried to throw, it didn't work.

Psalm 34:17 *declares When the righteous cry for help, the Lord hears and delivers them out of all their troubles.*

Her going through was merely a development process to take her to a higher level in God. Because she said Yes to the will of the Lord and understood that walking a straight and narrow path to live righteous before God, she had to count up the cost and prepare for the attacks ahead. For every spiritual level came new devils. Each time God raised her up and called her for new assignments, the enemy was present.

Ephesians 6:12 *For we do not wrestle against flesh and blood, but against the rulers, against the authorities, against the cosmic powers over this present darkness, against the spiritual forces of evil in the heavenly places.*

Because she ran on foot with men and stayed in the race without fainting or giving up. God saw her trustworthy enough to compete an even greater work. He kept elevating her higher and higher and taking her from Glory to Glory.

Chapter 7

*Stepping into Another Realm
Kingdom Labor*

By 1997, God stirred the nest again and had advanced her into another level and dimension in ministry. He never allowed her to get too comfortable. Her ministerial path had journeyed into another realm. So many doors had opened, and years of petitioned prayers had begun to manifest. After many years of being single since her first marriage, my mom patiently waited and believed God to send her a husband. She was never eager or hasty and never needed a man to complete her, she was made complete in God. She possessed the characteristics of a virtuous woman and was prepared to take on the responsibilities as a wife.

October 11, 1997 God answered her heart's desire and blessed her with a husband. She remained faithful at Glory Ministries until her marriage to Bishop Jessie James Toney where she joined him as a tag team in ministry as co-pastor. He had also served in ministry and is a man after

God's own heart. After being ordained by her husband, she became Pastor at Temple of Love and Truth.

God continuously advanced her for the work. When she entered this elevation, she was fully prepared and equipped. During her time as pastor, she was able to come off her job of many years and work full time in ministry. She held annual women's conferences, workshops, weekly intercessory prayer, trained women in ministry, provided marriage counseling and led by example of how to be a Godly woman. She provided faith-based resources that activated dormant potentials and so much more. During her personal time, she would go to the church daily to pray or clean just as she had always done. That routine never altered.

Due to her advancements she connected with so many other women in ministry that allowed her to build lasting relationships. Like an eagle, she extended her wings and soared touching lives of hundreds of people in her path. She had been assigned to an obligation to win souls, preach salvation, set the captives free, love on the members and tell them what thus said the Lord. Her spiritual intellect was depended upon by so many people for guidance. As a leader in the ministry, she desired that no one perish but to see souls encounter a relationship with Christ. Her loving spirit was a magnet to those who were spiritually lost. The path she led was holy which eagerly led so many others on a straight and narrow path. My mom was a trailblazer.

As a leader, she was held accountable for spiritual structure within the church. She began having intercessory prayer on Saturday mornings which became consistent for many years. The church doors would be open for those to come in pray and get what they needed from God. She never got tired praying and interceding, standing in the gap and staying on the wall until the prayers were manifested. She was an intercessor. Till this day, the members still continue to have intercessory prayer. Prayer has always been the foundation.

My sisters and I later joined our mom at Temple of Love and Truth to be under her leadership. She was not only recognized as our mother, but also admired as our Pastor. Yes, we were "Preacher Kids". Sitting under the wings of my mom's teaching, I witness a groundbreaking anointing and spiritual elevation in her. I saw Power. I witnessed God's Glory and His presence. I gained full understanding of higher levels and dimensions of the spirit realm. Whenever she had a prophetic word, it would be under the authority of the Holy Ghost and that with power. If she was instructed to speak a word from the Lord, she was obedient, she didn't hold back. My mom was courageous in operating in the ministry of deliverance. As a visionary and seer her gift brought revelation of prophetic accuracy. She had such a keen spiritual discernment that would dismantle any unclean spirit. She wasn't so hasty to lay hands on people; but she knew instantly when it was time to go into spiritual warfare. Often went toe to toe with the enemy, casting the enemy back into a dry place to die. But she was cover by the blood of Jesus. One thing she did not allow, was the enemy sitting up boldly in God's house. She had labored and prayed too much for the enemy to think he had free reign. The enemy had to flee.

Where the spirit of the Lord is there is liberty. One thing for sure, the presence of God dwelled wherever she had labored. She refused to be bound and weighed down. God was glorified for every operation of her spiritual gifts.

Chapter 8

The Annual Conference Impartation

Pastor Lucille Toney started her first women's conference in 2006. Talking about a life-changing experiences for many. My God! what started out as a conference for only the women each year it evolved into a conference for both men and women. She had a desire to see everyone partake in the blessings of the Lord. We anticipated the coming of the conference each year because we expected to see the move of God perform supernatural signs, miracles and wonders. There would be such a powerful breakthrough of the anointing spiritual needs of the people were met, some were delivered, set free, healed and others may have experienced a Godly connection and so much more. The conference had become a radical move of God.

Prophetic words of knowledge or confirmation spoken through God, were deposited into the people. She was always sensitive to the spirit and used wisdom while operating in the prophetic ministry. The more she stayed behind the veil in the presence of God, the more connected she had become with Him. Her kingdom work was to glorify God, and only moved when instructed by Him to do so.

One particular conference I'd never forget; a spiritual impartation were being imparted to those who were ready to receive it. To understand impartation, you must understand the anointing. So many spiritual gifts, blessings, healings, the gift of tongues and special endowments of power for the work of ministry were imparted into different ones. The glory of the Lord filled the room and the anointing was so powerful there was a certain sound from heaven that proceeded the move of God.

I witnessed several people being slain in the spirit, different ones running around the church praising God, some were worshipping, crying out before God, and laid out at the altar. Deliverance was going forth. Endless blessings from heaven were released. There was a sudden shift in the atmosphere as the Shekinah glory had filled the temple. We knew we were in the presence of the Lord. The spirit of God moved in a different way than ever before. No one left in the same manner they came.

The conference was so transforming for me, I felt a shift in my spirit and I received spiritual impartation. I was changed from that moment on and knew there was an urgency for me to absorb and study the word of God for myself. I remember sharing with my mom about my spiritual transformation, and my reading experiences while studying the word of God.

Many people benefited enormously through the conference and lives were tremendously impacted. Several people left understanding their purpose and many other ministerial journeys were birthed. Through it all, God was gloried. Purpose achieved!

Chapter 9

Well Done My Servant
Passing the Mantle

Train up a child in the way he should go when he is old he will not depart from it. **Proverbs 22:6,** My mother was the root to my foundation in having a strong prayer life. The more I would hear her prayers going forth; the more I listened, the more I witness divine advances; the more I thirst, the more my faith increased; the more inquisitive I had become. Many levels of spiritual impartations were planted; for me, it was nurturing and equipping me for a season such as this.

Because of the connection and kinship to who my mom was in God and to whose authority she operated under, I trusted her covering. I was trained at an early age.

I am equipped, as the fruit of that tree it's my duty to continue to carry the mantle that was passed. It is time to work and fulfill God's purpose, for only what we do for Christ will last. There is still a work to do.

The bible declares; ***Matthew 9:37-38,*** *The harvest is plentiful, but the workers are few. Therefore, beseech the Lord of the harvest to send out workers into His harvest.*

God's will override the will of our own any day. He is the creator and therefore we must trust His will for our lives. As a selfless faithful woman of God in ministry, my mom continued to intercede for others even during her illness while believing God for her healing. While on her bed of affliction, her faith stayed strong, she remained prayerful and still trusted God. I will never forget the words she deposited, saying "whatever you do stay with God and Keep Moving Forward". Before she transitioned, she had imparted a spiritual mantle into each of her daughters to anoint the birth of spiritual authority.

They say apples don't fall too far from the tree, well we are her fruit. We will continue to carry the torch she lit and blaze the trails she walked. Although we were clothed spiritually, her departure left us naturally naked; the covering that we adhered to had been lifted. Yet she left here knowing we were fully equipped for the kingdom work ahead. God had other levels of Kingdom ministry for her to fulfill therefore, she left no work here undone. She completed the assignment.

I am blessed beyond measure to have had a mother who was saved and lived a life pleasing to God.

Matthew 25:23 *Well done my good and faithful servant.*

Your labor was not in Vain!

Spiritual Mantles she passed on to her daughters

Chekita………………………………… The Overseer

Shuronda……………………………… The Prayer Warrior

Monica………………………………… The Demonstrator

Miriam………………………………… The Nurturer

My goal for writing this book, was to share my mother's ministry path as a dedicated faithful servant to God. She often voiced writing a book about her spiritual journey. Little did I know the task would have been assigned to me to fulfill. This read is not intended to glorify man in any form, but that God be glorified.

Throughout the context of this book, you will notice how I shifted from Pastor Lucille Toney to referencing her as my mom. This was intentionally written to honor her calling as a Pastor and still acknowledge her as my mom.

From Glory to Glory

A Word to Stand On-

Excerpts from original notes written by my mom

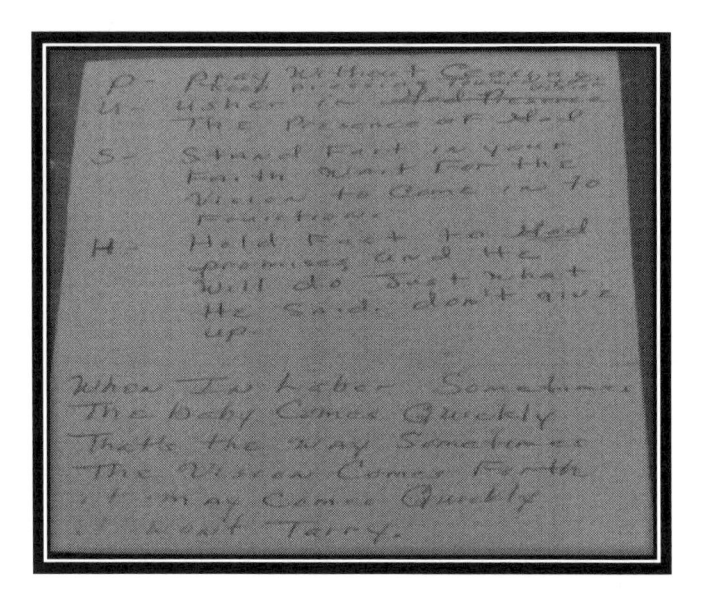

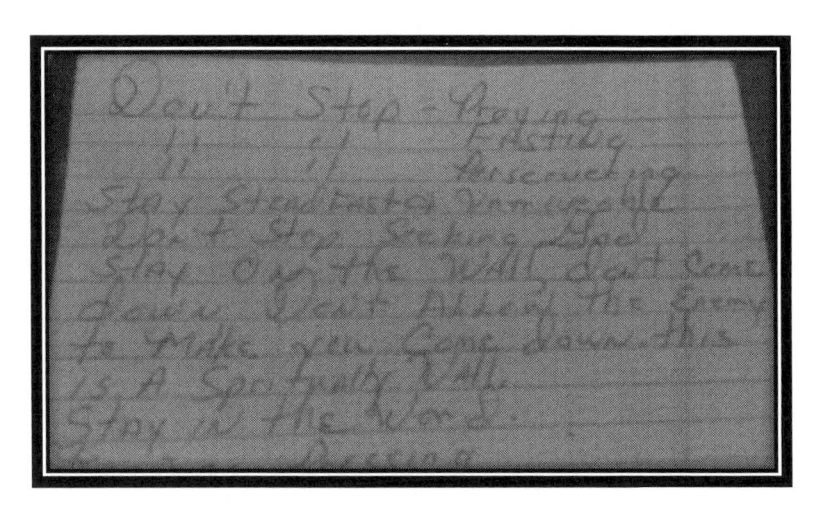

From Glory to Glory

Excerpts from original notes written by my mom

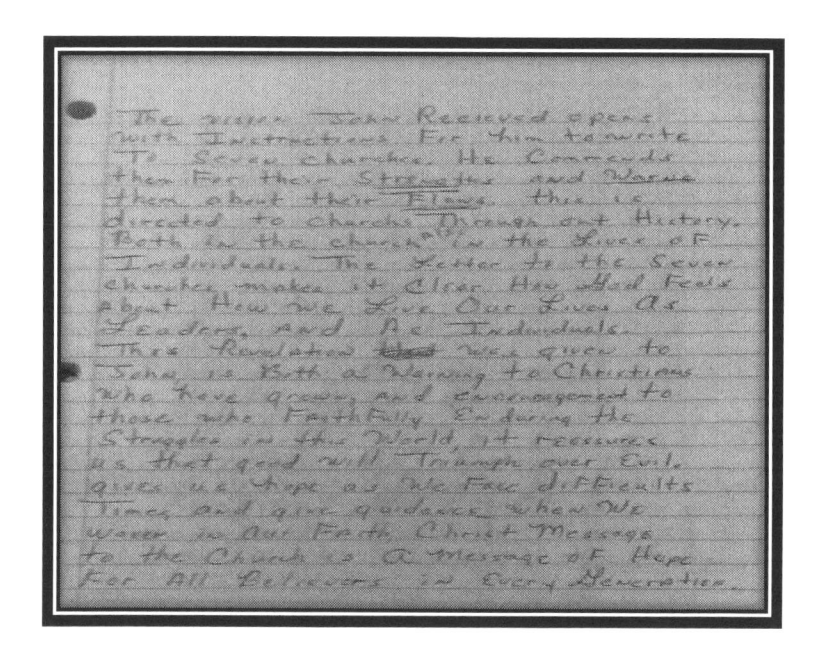

> The vision John Received opens with Instructions For him to write To Seven churches. He Commends them For their Strengths and Warns them about their Flaws. This is directed to churchs Through out History. Both in the church & in the Lives of Individuals. The Letter to the Seven churches, makes it clear How God Feels about How we Live Our Lives as Leaders, and As Individuals. This Revelation that was given to John is Both a Warning to Christians who have grown, and Encouragement to those who Faithfully Enduring the Struggles in this World, it reassures us that good will Triumph over Evil. gives us hope as We Face difficult Times and give guidance when we waver in our Faith. Christ Message to the Church is a message of Hope For All Believers in Every Generation.

> Message to the Seven Churches
>
> Church of Ephesus - this Church was Commended For their Hardwork and Perseverance, they were Rebuke For Forsaken their First Love. God told the Church to Repent (The Loveless Church)
>
> Church of Smyrna - This Church Suffered Persecution & Poverty. This Church had no Rebuke. He told this church Don't Fear Be Faithful (The Persecuted Church)
>
> Church of Pergamum - they were Commended By Being True to Faith they were Rebuke, Because they Compromise - God told this Church To Repent (The Compromising Church)
>
> Church of Thyatira - this Church were Commended, Because of their Love, Faith & Service they were Rebuke Because of immorality. God told this Church to Repent Because of that Jezebel who Calls her Self a Prophet - to Lead my Servant astray. (The Corrupt Church)

From Glory to Glory

Excerpts from original notes written by my mom

From Glory to Glory

Excerpts from original notes written by my mom

The Blood of Jesus

There is nothing as important then the Blood of Jesus which he Shed for the Sins of the People. His Blood is the most Precious Gift than any one could give. His Blood Brings Cleansing, His Blood Put us in right Standing with Him. What can make us holy, nothing But the Blood of Jesus. His Blood makes us Righteous. His Blood Put us in Covenant with Him. His Blood Can't be Taken For Granite. When we Partake of His Supper, and Eating of His body, we drinking of His blood which was Shed for the Forgiveness of Sin. The Blood is a Bond Between Him and the People that have Chosen to be in Covenant with Him. The Blood of Christ is Forever the Only means of a right Relationship with a Holy God. The Blood is our Weapon Against Satan. When we are in Covenant with Jesus, When We Call on the Name of Jesus He Just Sees Only the Blood, that is why we Say God Cover me in your Blood and Hide me Behind your Cross.

Morning Glory

He that dwelleth in the secret place of the most High shall abide under the shadow of the Almighty. **Psalms 91** Imagine being in a place of consecration where you are being shaped and molded and saturated in God's Glory. A place where His Holy Spirit overtakes every sense of your own understanding. A place where He directs your path and order your steps and you literally walk by faith and not by sight. A place where your mind is renewed and all you sense is the anointing of the Holy Spirit and His presence protecting your borders.

You become sensitive to His spirit as you began to take on His spirit. You witness levels, dimensions and higher heights in God. That's His desire, for us to allow Him to have free reign and elevate our spiritual being. Just as the bloom of morning glories. If we do not water our circumstances with the word of God, we wither.

Like the dew that rests, joy must eventually come in the morning to revive us. After the sleepless nights of torment, peace must eventually pass by my street in the morning. The enemy is busy everyday all day, but he works in overdrive at night.

It's ok; because we as Christians recognizes the swiftness of the attacks and we should be just as swift to Pray, be unmovable and remain in faith. A night of trouble doesn't last always because the morning brings Glory!

Acknowledgements

To my husband Bill and my kids MaCaerius and Braylan. Thank you for your constant love and support. I love you all

To my sisters Chekita, Shuronda, and Monica, my contributing authors. Thank you all for your support along the way in sharing our mother's spiritual journey. This book would not have been possible without your guidance. Love you much!

My sister Kim and my brothers Phalon and Ben thank you for always supporting my writing projects and believing in me. I love you.

To my mom's husband Bishop Jessie James Toney, Pastor Debra Johnson and the members of Temple of Love and Truth, thank you all so very much for your love support and keeping my mother's memory alive. She was truly dedicated to her church and had a special love for the members.

My aunt Jean I thank God for your guidance during my writing process. Your help was truly appreciated.

To my aunts and uncles and family thank you for your love and prayers.

Acknowledgements

To Apostle Eunice Holman (My Aunt Eunice) of Glory Ministries, where do I begin, you were a huge part of this project. Thank you so very much for being available whenever I called. Your input was valuable.

Jessie Robinson, thank you for being willing to help and provide insight. Your guidance was truly needed and appreciated.

Evelyn McGarity, thank you for your prayers over the years.

Pastor Cassandra Burse of Overseer at New Beginnings Christian Center, thank you so much for your love and continuous encouragement.

Pastor Jessie and Lashardra Toney of Agape International Healing Ministries, Thank you for your love, prayers, encouragement and constant support.

Acknowledgements

To all my nieces, thanks for your encouragement and support. Auntie love you.

Carol Jackson, my mom's BFF and true friend. Thank you for always being available. I appreciate your love, prayers and support through the years.

Pastor Ronnie and Celeste Toney of Brighter Day Word Ministry, Thanks for your love, prayers and constant support.

Minister Roshundia Tate of After the Pain Ministry, thank you for your love, prayers and support.

Rev. Panisha Stigger of New Hope Outreach, thank you for you love, prayers and support.

Tomesha Mitchell, thank you for your constant support and always being present when needed.

Minister Latina Chaney, thank you sis for your love, prayers and support.

Moneeka Marable, thank you sis for your kindness and simply always being supportive.

Shirley Jackson, you are a gem, thank you for your kindness.

Acknowledgements

Greta Webber thank you for your support "My Help".

Ms. Ora Smith, thank you for your love and prayers.

Ms. Sandra Alexander thank you for your love and prayers.

 Thanks to everyone who have been a part of my writing journey as well as a huge part of my mother's spiritual walk. Thank you for all your love, support, prayers and continuous encouragement through the years. I love and appreciate each of you.

Pastor & Prophetess Lucille Toney

About The Author

My name is Miriam Cauley-Crisp; I am a native of Memphis, Tennessee. I am the mother of two handsome boys MaCaerius and Braylan, whom I love dearly. I am a loving wife to my wonderful husband Bill whom I adore.

I am a saved God-fearing woman who loves the Lord; and accredits Him for all blessings He has bestowed upon my life.

I am a successful published author of two poetry books entitled ***"Through The Eyes of Mine" and "I Am My Poetry Heart and Soul"***.

Deuteronomy 28 Blessed

Let's Stay Connected

To contact the author or leave reviews please email
Miriamdcauley@gmail.com

For book purchases
https://www.paypal.me/MiriamCauley/12

Notes

From Glory to Glory

Notes

From Glory to Glory

Made in the USA
Columbia, SC
01 December 2023